Table of Contents

$he knows How To Get a Bag

Dedication

I dedicate this book to my family. My husband, Jay I love you and I appreciate your love for me and always believing and seeing what I see. No matter how crazy it might seem. How early it might come to me. You are always down for whatever and I love that! To my children, Ava and J2 you are the light to my darkness. Thank you for leading mommy to the correct way. To my grandmother Little Dot the storm is almost over! Thank you for always believing in me and encouraging me to go forth in my journey. To my great grandmother Big Dot, I love you and you are my reason! You are all my reason! I will never give up the race until I end statistics for you! To my grandmothers This book is dedicated to you!

With love !

-Mommy

Chapter 1 Nothing

Growing up poor and seeing my parents really struggle to make things happen for my siblings and I wasn't easy. Having to worry about where the next meal and roof for our heads would be tomorrow was tough. I promised myself and my mama we wouldn't live like that anymore. At an early age I already had my mind made up. I was going to do something successful to take care of my family. Although my mother was a hard worker she had fallen sick and it was all up to my step dad. Although he did a great job making sure we had what we needed. We had just moved back to Los Angeles. It wasn't easy, but we managed. Mama had gotten diagnosed with rheumatoid arthritis and was experiencing life at her worst. From staying with family members to staying with family friends. We had no one to turn to, no one on site or mind that we knew could help us get on our feet. We had used up all of our resources. God sent angels from unexpected places to get us by and Thank God they were willing to his word.

Once I had my own family getting a bag turnt all the way to another level. I began coming up with many solutions, researching a lot of different things I wanted to know more about. I became interested in fashion and makeup at an early age. Make sure your work space is doing what you love. When you love your hustle you will have more good days than bad days. What I went through as a child and what I experienced through my life all the way to adulthood built my character to grind. It helped me to understand that the beautifulest diamonds blossom from pressure.

Without money it is hard to maintain life. Many people achieve the goal of getting a bag. Many do crazy things to get a bag as well. Although this is the 21st century, making money can be really easy for most who put their mind to achieving this goal.

Chapter 2 Adulthood

I began learning about money at a young age. I learned that money was/is the root of all evil. That you need money to survive in this world. The currency of a dollar is very high today. I had to learn the hard way, money does not grow on trees LOL. If a man does not work (money) he does not eat. After graduating high school I went to college. Everyday I went to class and work and was one of those freshman who gained the fresh 40, because you miss home. Everything you eat as a freshman is fast food, noodles, or hot hunny buns w/ vanilla ice cream. Or was it just my roomies and I? Whatever the case maybe I hated it and I missed everything about my life. I had to secure a bigger bag that would allow me to do anything I wanted or needed to do. I moved back home and began life with my now husband. On our journey to marriage we taught each other many hustles and ways to secure the bag.

As a couple we've built each other up more and more and learned from each other's lives of what we don't want to repeat with our own family. Breaking the cycle and creating a smooth path for our children. If you do not have children pick a bigger cause other than yourself to make you go harder than normal. (Example-family/community/someone who has supported you)

The 4 keys to success is to:

- Never limit yourself to what you can do!

- Always tell yourself and your doubters you can and

  you WILL DO IT!

- Stick to your purpose!

- Pray through it all Good/Bad!

- Consistency

Nothing in this world is given for free, there's a price for everything. Yes you will go through trials! Yes you will go through tribulations! It is up to you and your character to determine how and if you will come out on top. Create a plan, stick to your plan, and T.K.A!

Life is full of blessings, but life is also full of lessons. Take everything as a lesson and learn from it for future obstacles. Life is what you make it and ownership is great!

<u>Success</u>

what people think
it looks like

<u>Success</u>

what it really
looks like

Formula :

Plan + Determination + Test – Failure = Success

Chapter 3 Adulthood-Love

Love is good. Love is sweet. Love can be dangerous. Love can be bent. Love can be painted. Love can be tainted. Love can be wild. Love is a lesson. Love is a blessing. You said you love me? Well that's just great let's move together and stay together. Love forever and apart never. Love me! All of me, until the end. Multiply and never sin.

I met my husband when I was eighteen years old, at a summer job in Los Angeles, CA. We went on a blind date with our friends and didn't know that night would be the night that set our future up with each other. I remember my husband taking me home after our date and stopping to get gas at a gas station near the restaurant. Upon getting in his car I asked was he a gangbanger lol, because I needed to know before getting in the car. He laughed and said "no get in the car you're safe." I remember joking with him telling him that I was too much for him to handle. He laughed and said "yea right." We both laughed and then he grabbed my face, stole a kiss and jumped out of the car to grab gas. Leaving me speechless and in a daze. I glance at my friend in the other car beside us and see her laughing and saying yea! Still speechless and in a daze I snapped out of it and began to smile because I couldn't believe that had just happened to me. I didn't say anything else just rode home laughing to myself because I was still in shock. I am pretty sure he saw that crazy smirk on my face trying to disguise a straight face. He became my lover, best friend, soul mate, husband, and father of our two beautiful children.

Chapter 3 Children are Sweet! Children are Kind!

Children are the future of our world. As a parent you grow instinct to give your children whatever they want. No one ever said having kids would be easy or that it would be hard either. You never know what you're getting yourself into until you're already waist deep. Being broke and growing up not really having much. Hustle, Hustle, Hustle was all I knew when it came to securing the bag. I had my mind made up already that my kids would never experience what I experienced as a child sleeping from pillow to post and watching my parents stress at their lowest about money. God had blessed us with two beautiful blessings and not securing the bag was totally out of the question. Not only was securing the bag a main priority. Poverty was not! Giving them a life I didn't have was the only option I had for myself and my children. Sometimes you have to completely step out of your comfort zone and do what is needed to

get your bag like a boss.

Everyone should experience poverty at least 1 or 2 times out

of their life. It will teach you survival through a different perspective.

You will meet many people that will share their story on how they

got to the point they are in, in their life. Everyone's story is different

and has a different ending. Are you strong enough to make it

through with a successful ending? If you don't have children, what is

your drive?

Even if you aren't ready to invest in yourself invest into companies that

care about you and your investment. Work for a company that loves

your ethic, the way you work, and if you will stay or move forward with

your journey to success.

Chapter 4 If all fails get that bag …

You are going to face a lot throughout your journey of life. Everyone will, no one is perfect and life is full of life learned lessons. Your purpose is to secure the bag by all means necessary. Your Broke?, Husband/Man ain't acting right?, Kids stressing you out? Bills becoming too High?, Wanna vacation?, Want to take yourself out, but don't have the funds? Girl go get that bag! Remember anytime life gets too hard pray and trust that God will always see you through and bring you through all the obstacles that you are facing. Life would not be life without the constant obstacle that teaches us to endure it all. Pressure creates diamonds. Girl go get that bag! Keep pressing, success is near and you're close to the finish line! You got this!

Formula: Pressure + Stone = Diamond = Money Bag

Chapter 5 The Hardest Part

Life is honestly like a box of chocolates you never know what your going to get, it's scary I KNOW! Understand that God will never put you through more than you can handle. Take a deep breathe and believe with everything in you that you could make it and PRAY.

- Strategize- devise a strategy or strategies
- Test- reveal the strengths or capabilities of someone or something by putting them under strain

Things will always happen out of your control, continue to press and move forward. No matter how much it happens. Remember test=testimony, what will be your testimony? Create a vision board to get an idea and plan for yourself.

Things Needed:

White board/project poster board

Lots of Magazines

Scissors

Glue

Set aside an hour, grab a glass of wine and let's brainstorm!

Set 2 goals for yourself one short term goal and one long term goal.

Your short term goal being a goal that you want to accomplish soon.

Your long term goal is something you want to work on achieving, but

you are giving yourself a longer time to complete this goal. When

setting these goals be realistic you want to really achieve everything

on your vision board. Ready. Set. Paste! Life will give you lemons,

make lemonade and GET THAT BAG SIS! Period! Never forget to

Pray.

There will always be many people that you will encounter that may not

be happy about what you are doing or your accomplishments. You have to

continue on your mission to complete your task. Hop the obstacle with your

best stance and know that you have got this! Say a small prayer and focus on

what the ending will be once you have completed! I know. IT'S HARD! Nothing

is too hard without God, pray!

When doing something positive, things will always happen to make

your positive turn negative. Stay focused and understand that this is only temporary. Have a back up plan just in case your plan doesn't go as planned, so that your umbrella is near during your short storm.

Life is all about lessons, what you choose to do with your lessons will determine the type of person you are, what you can handle, and your future. Do not let the things that you are going through temporarily affect your life permanently. Be stronger than your thoughts and get that bag sis!

Chapter 6 #Pray

Life will bring you many ups and downs, you have to determine if you will own your life or will your life own you. God gives us decisions to make and allows us to choose what we feel is best for our situation. PRAY! Before making any moves consider God in your daily routine. He talks back, believe me! When you least expect it listen with your mind, body, and soul. Once you have received your sign allow God to move in your situation. Prayer really works. PRAY!

Prayer to Say For Situation

God thank you for allowing me to reach it this far in my journey. Please guide my footsteps that will allow me to pass this test. I know nothing is too big or too hard for you to handle. I am casting all my worries and fears to you. Allow me to get through this journey with favor so that I can surpass expectations. To be able to help those in need around me and forever be a blessing to those who are true of need. To always remember where you brought me from and never lose my way.

Amen.

Once you see your work starting to progress and blossom there will be things to go wrong on your journey. Keep faith and continue to pray through this process. Bad happens before good to insure you are ready for what's to come. Stay focused! You're only a step away from your finish line. Keep pressing until you see your manifestation.

Prayer to say for manifestation

God thank you for the blessings I have received and the blessings that are on the way. Cover me as I walk down this path of success. Allow me to connect with the right people that will connect me to my mission. Allow my hard work to continue to manifest and blossom all the way out. Thank you for the experiences. Thank you for the lessons. Allow me to stand every time I fall. Allow me to get back up and continue this race. Allow me to greatly reap what I have sowed into my bag. Allow it to runneth over for me. Thank you for allowing me to experience this manifestation in my life. Amen

Work and progress will only allow you to get better and better at what you do. Drive and passion will take you far. Don't stop now, continue the race your manifestation is on its way.

Chapter 7 Let's Make This Money

Every trial has tribulations, if I told you making money was easy I would be lying to you. I will tell you there are some easy ways to achieve this goal. Get determined about something and flip it into an investment. If you like makeup, become a makeup artist or brand your own makeup line and sell it to other makeup lovers. If you like hair become a hair stylist or brand your own hair care products and sell your brand. If you like clothing, become a wardrobe consultant/ personal stylist. If you are a social media fanatic, become a blogger. Make sure you're comfortable and love the job that you are working. This will insure your success because you are comfortable making money in your space.

Now that you are comfortable in your space, how will you make more money? Invest your time into the things you want to invest your money into. Have a plan, work it out and play out your cause and effects.

So that no matter what you have a plan and are prepared for whatever outcome you may have in the end.

Numbers show results, what do you see? Is it worth your time, money, and effort? If not maybe it is not the trade for you. Adding your numbers together will result in your progression. What do your numbers say? What will you do with the money you have made?

A. Invest and Save!

B. Invest and Save!

C. Invest and save!

D. All of the above

Invest and save! Yes that is correct!

If you got the question correct, you are on the path to success. Keep pushing towards your ultimate goal. Securing the bag sis! You are almost there to finish your race!

Chapter 8 24/8

There are 24 hours in a day; everyone has the same amount of hours. What he/she chooses to do with those hours determines a person's ability to get money. Make everyday count, what can you do to make your life successful?

What could you do daily to improve your life and money bag skills? Job, start an entrepreneurship, surveys, make a resume, or etc. Whatever your trade is, make every day better than your last doing what you love and flipping it into money. Have a plan. Proceed with your plan six months plus. Pray through the process before hand, during hand, and after. Never forget God as your assistant through this process. "A man that does not work does not eat…"

Lifestyle of one should be to have fun, enjoy life, while making money continuously. Things happen for a reason. Everyone's story is different, what will your story be? Where do you want to see yourself in six months?

Chapter 9 Who Are you?

I look in the mirror often and I perfect my imperfections. Who we are is who God already branded us to be as a whole. We cannot change that unless altered. I am a mother, wife, daughter, sister, entrepreneur, fighter, C.O.G, and etc. Who are you?

People will always make up their own perspective of who they believe you to be, but who are you really? That is all up to you to determine the true validity of their perspective of you or to just leave it as their opinion. Whatever you do, do not allow them to alter your mission of getting your bag! People will always talk let them. If you aren't the topic you aren't doing something right.

Who we are is all up to US. I would rather live for something rather than dying for nothing. Everyday is a new opportunity to make today better than yesterday. You can either be successful or disappointed in your progression. Who you are determines your future. Who are you?

You will experience a lot during your life that will test your character. Do not give up no matter how hard your journey may seem. With every goal you set for yourself, set a reward aside to give to yourself for celebration. Just picture yourself running through that red tape to receive your prize. Can you feel the adrenaline? That's how winning feels.

Project

Things needed:

1 notebook

2 different color ink pens

5 sticky notes

Instructions:

Make a list of things you need to accomplish for the month that you are currently in, break these tasks up into a four week period. Each day of the week have a goal jotted down for each day. When that day approaches and you have completed your assigned goal, mark the day with a green check. Green means GO! You're going and moving closer to your ultimate goal. Once you have completed your goals for the week write the word completed or words of encouragement to show that you can are on the right path. For example: "You go girl!", "You did it!"

Let's work!

Monday	Tuesday	Wednesday	Thursday	Friday	Saturday	Sunday
-create logo for business ✓	-create a business plan ✓	-do natural styles on hair ✓	-record a youtube video ✓	-write lyrics to song ✓	-create your own blog ✓	COMPLETED YOU GO GIRL! GOALS COMPLETED!

Chapter 10 Energy

Energy has a big impact on a person's daily livelihood. The energy a person receives can cause happy or negative vibes. These vibes can add or subtract from your overall energy levels causing you to be mad, happy, or sad.

Energy a degree or level of energy possessed by something or required by a process. I believe the vibes that a person gives determines if they are good / bad for you. Negative energy causes drain of your energy. Be sure to protect your energy by all means necessary! God will allow you to see the negative from the positive sometimes. As the temple you have to protect and allow your temple to be at peace.

Manage the people you surround yourself with on a daily

basis. This has the biggest impact on your daily energy. You need to

be able to have 100% energy to be successful in getting that bag sis!

The energy received by people around you everyday can also

affect your energy levels. Having bad energy meaning always

negative, never happy for anyone else, doesn't have anything going

on for themselves. This is all signs of negative energy.

Evaluate everything that you put your energy towards and

determine if it will add or subtract from your bag. Being alert and

ahead of the game can help you alot in the end. Just remember

anything negative will subtract, and anything positive will add.

Chapter 11 Do It!

You will never be ready! So just do it! Execute your plan and improve as you go! Many people have a hard time bringing their plan to life because they are too busy trying to prepare the best. Yes this is great, sometimes it's better to present what you have and improve as you go. This will give great practice and less stress! Many great entrepreneurs had a plan that they executed and failed, this gave them the strength to continue and improve all known errors to insure a successful retry.

It's okay to step out on faith! What's the worst that could happen? You've made it this far! You are an entrepreneur! Everyday is a new day to better your yesterday. Do you want to live for something? Or Die for nothing? What is your drive? Put that energy towards your bag and push it to the limit. #DOIT

Here's a great way to keep track of your progress and to become stronger and more confident in your business.

Things needed:

-Monthly planner

- Pen

- Highlighters (different colors)

- Calendar

-Schedule

Project – Complete a week agenda of things that you can do everyday differently to improve your business. Once completed for the week everyday that you complete highlight all your important tasks with one color and the least important things in another color. This will make it a bit exciting and not so much as homework. As you complete your days this week mark out your day completed with a red pen. In this assignment red means good! All reds mean you have completed your daily task and are closer and closer to getting that bag sis!

For example :

-Monday- Name my business/Get business license

-Tuesday- Brand my business

M	T	W	TH	F	S	S
-lose 10 pounds	-go to Office Depot	-go to the gym	-work on business plan	-sketch out plan	strategize business plan	-Rest

Chapter 12 A SECRET

I believe in luck sometimes and I believe that some things that are very important deserve privacy. Many times we can be so excited about our ideas, accomplishments, or goals that we just want to share with others to express our excitement. This is great, hold it in a little bit longer to complete all necessary tacks. While support is the best feeling from those close to you. Many people will disappoint you during this journey due to jealousy and negativity. A finish is always better than an almost. Complete your set goals and brag to your loved ones and friends once you have completed those short term goals and can see the outcome to show the results. (For example: lost 10 pounds/ completed college / started a new business etc.) This gives no room to allow any negativity in your space.

Continue to press forward and move in silence. Your paper is your greatest revenge. Things that you are working on will sound so much better with proof as evidence. All work no play! Save your

money, spend only what you will need. The things that you totally

want can wait.

Chapter 13 God is Real ….

I remember really going through hard and tough times, and really just sitting puzzled like okay what does this mean God? Why am I going through this, in this time of my life or even at all? Like this can't be real. Then a thought in my head flashes "In order to get somewhere you have to take a route." There may be wrecks, cars on fire, people in the street, anything that can stop you on your way to your destination. In life you have to go through something to get somewhere. Meaning you may have distractions and disappointments on your way, but never let that stop you from going where you need to go. Don't stray away from your route, there is no map on this journey.

Now is the time to Get That Bag Sis! The only thing that matters the most at this moment. Who's to say you won't experience the worst? Who's to say you will make it to your

destination fast without any distractions or disappointments? Only

yourself and God. Keep following your route and focus on your

destination.

Chapter 14 Get That Bag Sis!

To have a successful business and succeed in getting that bag you have to have a plan. Be sure to create your plan starting off with a product, a name, and a plan to execute how you will get that bag! Time is ticking and it's never too late to start something that will benefit your name and what you stand for as a whole! What sets you apart from others around you makes you different. You are an entrepreneur embrace your skin and get that bag sis!

Here are a couple of vendors to help those who may be stuck on a product. These vendors are all single picked and researched to insure the best quality product, shipping, and customer service. Choose the category that best fits your brand, complete your projects, create a plan, stick to it, and GET THAT BAG SIS!

Hair

Alimina Hair

Email- hair003@aliminahair.com

Jean Chen

+8613326491671

Suna Su

+8613822139457

Makeup

Winky Cosmetics

Maggie

Telephone number - +8675523035123

Yvonne Shi

+8613898674735

King Wang

+8615092166252

Candy

+8618028447851

Lipstick

Lily Lee

lily@xinlimeiindustry.com

Sophie Xie

+8618565663457

Fashion

Queen Moen

Sindy

https://m.queenmoen.com

Email- moendress@queenmoen.com

Belle Wholesale

www.bellewholesale.com

**Electronics**

Amy

Telephone number - 00861871886852

Vivian Zhang

Telephone number- +8615159055308

email- bjbj05@szenle.com

Sophie Liu

+8618923400616

CHAPTER 15 NO!

You will be told no a lot during this journey. Whatever you do, do not give up! There is always another way. Your research can only get broader when it comes to perfecting your business. Turn that NO into a YES and create a lane that you can control yourself. Shadow others who are doing the job you pursue, mimic their way and add your own twist. This will make those who doubted you notice your purpose. Understanding a NO is just a hold on! Don't believe it's the end of your career, use this as gas to amp up your ambition. The most successful person was told no 100 times before being told yes that's it! Only the real can survive! Every time you think about giving up just think about how far you have come and how much farther you have to go. Go hard or go home!

If I had a quarter for every no I have received in my life, I would honestly be rich without even trying. God will allow you to meet people in your life who will try to discourage you so that you will not continue your journey. Pray you make it through and keep your best foot forward. As long as you are progressing you are doing what you have planned. Meaning you are on track. Get that bag sis!

Chapter 16 Dedication Part II

I dedicate my story to that little girl who has fire in her Go, but is stuck in a time in her life where it seems like everything is against her. Hold on! You're almost to your destination. Hold on! Your journey shouldn't be long. Little girl you will soon be a woman one day, and you can then say I made it! Just hold on! Your journey won't be long. Remember this path so that when your sister is at rage at a stage in her life you can share this journey and say HOLD ON! I told you your journey wouldn't be long! Life can be unbearable but it ain't terrible! Focus on your path and you shall pass everyone in your way. Turn around and say hold on! My brother! My sister! Hold on! Your journey today is only a short way! Just hold on! This too shall pass! Even without a hall pass, you shall make it past all the hard ache and pain. Once your finished you can sit back and reminisce on all your memories from your journey and

say, I made it! Just hold on!

Thank you!

I hope you have enjoyed this book as much as I enjoyed writing it for you guys! I want to give a special thank you, to each and everyone of you who purchased this book! You are special! Know that you can do it! You're almost to the finish line, do not give up! If this race was easy anyone could do it. That is why we are special and with this map you will be led directly to your treasure of Gold. Get that bag sis!

Thank you for your support!

-Missy

What does that mean?

Moneybag/bag – a sack of money

Get that bag sis- get that money

Mimic- copy

Test- reveal the strengths or capabilities of someone or something by putting them under strain

Strategize- devise a plan or strategy

C.O.D- Child of God

Revenue- money earned from an investment

Energy- the strength and vitality required for sustained physical or mental activity.

LOL- Laugh out Loud

Hustle- to sell something aggressively

God- The creator and ruler of the universe and source of all moral authority; the supreme being.

Dedication- the quality of being dedicated or committed to a task or purpose.